T0352778

LOSE YOURSELF

By / Gan Katherine Chandler

CAST

Nate Aaron Anthony
Yaz Gabrielle Creevy
Josh Tim Preston

CREATIVE TEAM / TÎM CREADIGOL

Director / Cyfarwyddwr Patricia Logue
Designer / Cynllunydd Carla Goodman
Lighting Designer / Cynllunydd Goleuo Andy Pike
Sound Designer / Cynllunydd Sain Sam Jones
Choreographer / Coreograffydd Shekira Johnson
Deputy Stage Manager / Dirprwy Reolwr Llwyfan Amy Wildgoose
Assistant Stage Manager / Rheolwr Llwyfan Cynorthwyol Josie Allen

---

Lose Yourself was first performed at Sherman Theatre on 10 May 2019.
Perfformiwyd *Lose Yourself* yn gyntaf yn Theatr y Sherman ar 10 Mai 2019.

THE CREATIVE TEAM
TÎM CREADIGOL

KATHERINE CHANDLER *Writer / Awdur*

Katherine is an award-winning writer working in theatre, film and television and is Playwright in Residence at Sherman Theatre. She has twice been a finalist for the prestigious Susan Smith Blackburn Prize with *Before It Rains* (a Sherman Theatre and Bristol Old Vic co-production) and *Parallel Lines*, and was awarded the judges prize in the Bruntwood Prize for Playwriting for *Bird*. Co-produced by Sherman Theatre and Royal Exchange Theatre, *Bird* was the first collaboration between the two companies and received critical acclaim at national level. Her most recent play *Thick as Thieves*, co-produced by Clean Break and Theatr Clwyd also received critical acclaim nationally.

Katherine was the inaugural winner of the BBC Cymru Wales and National Theatre Wales, Wales Drama Award and has worked a number of times with both companies. BBC iPlayer released Katherine's first film, *Tag*, as part of the BBC3/BBC iPlayer drama launch. She has worked with BBC Drama on both *EastEnders* and *Casualty* and is currently working with them on a new project. Katherine's most recent works have been produced by companies including Sherman Theatre, Clean Break Theatre Company, National Theatre Wales, Theatr Clwyd, Manchester Royal Exchange Theatre, Bristol Old Vic and Nottingham Playhouse.

Mae Katherine yn awdur arobryn sy'n gweithio ym maes theatr, ffilm a theledu ac yn Ddramodydd Preswyl Theatr y Sherman. Mae wedi cyrraedd rownd derfynol gwobr fawreddog Susan Smith Blackburn gyda'i dramâu *Before it Rains* (cyd-gynhyrchiad rhwng Theatr y Sherman a Bristol Old Vic) a *Parallel Lines*. Dyfarnwyd gwobr y beirniaid i Katherine yng ngwobrau Bruntwood am ei drama *Bird*. Cafodd *Bird* ei chyd-gynhyrchu gan y Royal Exchange Theatre ym Manceinion a Theatr y Sherman, sef y cywaith cyntaf rhwng y ddau gwmni a chafodd ganmoliaeth drwy Brydain. Cafodd ei drama ddiweddaraf *Thick as Thieves*, a gyd-gynhyrchwyd gan Clean Break a Theatr Clwyd ganmoliaeth drwy Brydain hefyd.

Katherine oedd enillydd cyntaf Gwobr Drama Cymru y BBC Cymru Wales a National Theatre Wales, ac mae wedi gweithio gyda'r ddau gwmni nifer o weithiau. Rhyddhaodd BBC iPlayer ffilm gyntaf Katherine, *Tag*, fel rhan o lansiad drama BBC3/BBC iPlayer. Mae wedi gweithio gyda BBC Drama ar *EastEnders* a *Casualty*, ac ar hyn o bryd mae'n gweithio ar brosiect newydd gyda nhw. Mae gweithiau diweddaraf Katherine wedi'u cynhyrchu gan gwmnïau fel Theatr y Sherman, Cwmni Theatr Clean Break, National Theatre Wales, Theatr Clwyd, y Royal Exchange Theatre ym Manceinion, yr Old Vic ym Mryste a Nottingham Theatre.

PATRICIA LOGUE

Director / Cyfarwyddwr

Patricia Logue is an Associate Artist of Sherman Theatre. She trained in acting at The City University of New York and in voice at Royal Central School of Speech & Drama and is a lecturer in Acting at the Royal Welsh College of Music & Drama. Directing credits include – for Royal Welsh College of Music & Drama – *Thérèse Raquin*, *In the Next Room (The Vibrator Play)*, *Twelfth Night*, *Much Ado About Nothing* and *The Merchant of Venice* and *Not I* for Balance '16 and subsequently, Sherman Theatre. Patricia has also worked extensively as a text associate in theatre, film and television productions both in Ireland and the UK.

Mae Patricia Logue yn Artist Cyswllt Theatr y Sherman. Hyfforddodd mewn actio ym Mhrifysgol Dinas Efrog Newydd ac mewn llais yn y Royal Central School of Speech & Drama ac mae'n ddarlithydd Actio yng Ngholeg Brenhinol Cerdd a Drama Cymru. Mae ei llwyddiannau cyfarwyddo yn cynnwys – ar gyfer Coleg Brenhinol Cerdd a Drama Cymru – *Thérèse Raquin*, *In the Next Room (The Vibrator Play)*, *Twelfth Night*, *Much Ado About Nothing* a *The Merchant of Venice* a *Not I* ar gyfer Balance '16 ac yna, Theatr y Sherman. Mae Patricia wedi gweithio'n helaeth hefyd fel cydymaith testun mewn cynyrchiadau theatr, ffilm a theledu yn Iwerddon a Phrydain.

CARLA GOODMAN

Designer / Cynllunydd

Credits include / Credydau yn cynnwys: *Martha, Josie and the Chinese Elvis* (Stephen Joseph Theatre); *Don Juan Comes Back From The Way* (RADA); *Romeo & Juliet* (Orange Tree); *Wolves Are Coming For You* (Pentabus & Everyman Theatre); *Joy* (Stratford East); *Pride and Prejudice* (Nottingham Playhouse & York Theatre Royal); *Looking At Lucian* (Theatre Royal Bath); *Gabriel* (Richmond Theatre & UK Tour / Taith y DU); *Ariodante* (Royal Academy of Music); *Heartbreak Hotel* (The Jetty, Greenwich); *As the Crow Flies* (Pentabus & Salisbury Playhouse); *Miss Nightingale* (The Vaults); *How To Date A Feminist, Kitchen to Measure* (Arcola Theatre); *Rise* (Old Vic New Voices); *Jack and the Beanstalk* (Cast Theatre, Doncaster); *Miss Julie* (Etcetera Theatre); *Pig Farm* (St. James); *Truce* (New Wimbledon Theatre); *What Flows Past The Baltic* (Nottingham Playhouse); *Theatre Uncut* (Traverse Theatre & UK Tour / Taith y DU); *Listen, We're Family* (Wiltons Music Hall); *Much and Me* (Bush Theatre); *I Am Your Neighbour* (Oval House); *A New Face For Fast Times* (Soho Theatre); *The Love Project* (Arts Depot & UK Tour / Taith y DU); *Nola* (Underbelly, Edinburgh); *Step Live!* (Royal Academy of Dance & Southwark Centre); *Mr Happiness* (Old Vic Tunnels); *Bud Take The Wheel* (Shaw Theatre & Underbelly, Edinburgh).

ANDY PIKE

Lighting Designer / Cynllunydd Goleuo

Theatre includes / Theatr yn cynnwys: *Nutcracker* (Atlanta Ballet); *Company* (West End); *City of Dreams* (Ranger Productions); *Eye of The Storm* (Theatr na nÓg).

TV includes / Teledu yn cynnwys: *Strictly Come Dancing* (BBC).

Sports & Events include / Chwaraeon a Digwyddiadau yn cynnwys: Prince Charles' 70th Birthday Party; Handball World Cup; Asian Games.

SAM JONES

Sound Designer / Cynllunydd Sain

For Sherman Theatre / Ar gyfer Theatr y Sherman: *Woof*, *Fel Anifail*, *Tremor*, *The Motherfucker with the Hat* (& Tron Theatre), *The Weir* (& Tobacco Factory Theatres), *Iphigenia in Splott*, *Love Cardiff: City Road Stories*, *Arabian Nights, Home*, *Heritage* (Theatr Ieuenctid y Sherman / Sherman Youth Theatre), *All That I Am, Fe Ddaw'r Byd I Ben* (& The Richard Burton Company, Royal Welsh College of Music and Drama / Coleg Brenhinol Cerdd a Drama Cymru).

Other theatre includes / Theatr arall yn cynnwys: *Saethu Cwningod/ Shooting Rabbits* (PowderHouse); *Anweledig* (Frân Wen); *The Last Five Years* (Leeway Productions & Wales Millennium Centre); *Tuck* (Neontopia & WMC); *The Sinners Club* (Gagglebabble); *The Worlds Wife* (WNO); *Blackbird, St Nicholas, Sand* (The Other Room); *Richard iii Redux* (The Llanarth Group); *Looking Through Glass* (difficult|stage); *Light Waves Dark Skies, The Girl With The Incredibly Long Hair* (We Made This); *This Incredible Life* (Canoe Theatre Company); *Growth, Blue, Ring Ring* (The Richard Burton Company, RWCMD / CBCDC).

CAST

AARON ANTHONY *Nate*

 Theatre includes / Theatr yn cynnwys: *A View From The Bridge*, *Macbeth* (Tobacco Factory Theatres); *'Tis Unmanly Grief* (Theatre N16); *Twelfth Night*, *Billy Liar* (Royal Exchange Theatre, Manchester); *Human Emotional Process* (Chaskis & Arts Theatre); *Much Ado About Nothing* (Shakespeare's Globe); *Shakespeare In Love – The Play* (Disney); *The Last Days Of Mankind* (Bristol Old Vic).

TV includes / Teledu yn cynnwys: *Delicious* (Bandit Television/Sky); *Doctors*, *Holby City* (BBC); *Outlaws* (Hartswood Films); *Witless* (Objective).

Radio includes / Radio yn cynnwys: *Torchwood: God Among Us Part 3* (Big Finish).

GABRIELLE CREEVY *Yaz*

 Having graduated from Arts Educational in 2018, *Lose Yourself* marks Gabrielle's professional stage debut. / Ar ôl iddi raddio o Ysgol Berfformio ArtsEd Llundain yn 2018, *Lose Yourself* yw cynhyrchiad llwyfan proffesiynol cyntaf Gabrielle.

Theatre while training / Theatr wrth hyfforddi: *The Suicide*, *The Winter's Tale*, *Machinal*, *People*, *Places and Things* (Arts Educational).

TV includes / Teledu yn cynnwys: *15 Days* (Boom Cymru/Channel 5); *Casualty* (BBC); *The Stand Up Sketch Show* (Spirit Media); *In My Skin* (BBC Three pilot); *Gwaith/Cartref* (S4C).

TIM PRESTON *Josh*

 Theatre while training / Theatr wrth hyfforddi: *All That I Am* (Sherman Theatre & The Richard Burton Company, Royal Welsh College of Music and Drama / Coleg Brenhinol Cerdd a Drama Cymru); *Mojo*, *Saved*, *The London Cuckolds*, *The Taming of the Shrew* (The Richard Burton Company, RWCMD / CBCDC).

Theatre includes / Theatr yn cynnwys: *Peter Pan* (Regent's Park Open Air Theatre); *First Light* (Chichester Festival Theatre).

Film includes / Ffilm yn cynnwys: *Purge of Kingdoms* (Conglomerate Media).

TV includes / Teledu yn cynnwys: *Warren* (Hat Trick International); *The Barking Murders* (ITV); *Holby City* (BBC); *Goodnight Sweetheart* (Retort).

SHERMAN
THEATR • THEATRE

WELCOME
CROESO

Lose Yourself is our third piece of exciting new writing in spring 2019 exploring the world we live in right now and follows on from *Woof* and *The Taming of the Shrew*. I am delighted that both the writer and director of *Lose Yourself* are Associate Artists of Sherman Theatre. Katherine Chandler is an exceptional Welsh playwright creating important work for our times, and Patricia Logue is a hugely insightful director. We are delighted to share this important, powerful and poignant play with you, our audiences.

Lose Yourself yw'r trydydd darn o ysgrifennu newydd cyffrous yn nhymor y gwanwyn 2019 sy'n archwilio'r byd yr ydym ni'n byw ynddo yn nawr ac yn dilyn *Woof* a *The Taming of the Shrew*. Rydw i mor falch bod yr awdur a'r cyfarwyddwr yn Artistiaid Cyswllt i Theatr y Sherman. Mae Katherine Chandler yn ddramodydd rhagorol o Gymru sy'n creu gwaith pwysig ar gyfer ein hamseroedd, ac yn nwylo medrus Patricia Logue mae hwn yn argoeli i fod yn gynhyrchiad gafaelgar. Rydyn ni'n edrych ymlaen at gyflwyno'r gwaith pwerus ac ingol hwn gyda chi ein cynulleidfaoedd.

JULIA BARRY
Sherman Theatre Executive Director /
Cyfarwyddwr Gweithredol Theatr y Sherman

Way back in 2014, I wrote a monologue for a character called Yaz. She was going out clubbing with her mate Samantha and she needed something to wear. The play was a day and a night in her life. I wrote it quickly and then shelved it but kept going back to it and working with it. Over time I also became interested in the story from the perspective of the men Yaz met that night. In 2016 I had a conversation with Rachel O'Riordan about writing a play about a night out, about masculinity and women and lack of opportunity and sex and drink culture and football. *Lose Yourself* was commissioned.

KATHERINE CHANDLER

Writer / Awdur

It is always more thought-provoking to consider a character's actions – no matter how reprehensible – with an understanding of the social restrictions, triggering events and learned behaviour that might lead to them. *Lose Yourself* is at its best when these factors are considered. Katherine Chandler, without reducing the inexcusable nature of her characters' behaviour, encourages an observation of the social and environmental restrictions placed upon them. In doing so, she ensures an informed judgement from her audience.

Yaz is a product of her environment – an environment where opportunity is limited and solid structures for learning how to get ahead, existing successfully in an adult world and looking after herself haven't been in place. So naturally, her life choices reflect this. Nate's course of action throughout is a direct result of elemental, learned behaviour passed on to him in a professional sports environment rooted in sexism and misogyny. Josh, the youngest of the three and with a lot to lose, is wound up tight – ready to snap with the ongoing pressure of needing to escape his limited existence. He is easily triggered when presented with any obstacle that might endanger his route out. The characters are not without aspiration but the prevailing theme in the play of reduced opportunity, makes it difficult for them to fulfil these aspirations, or in Nate's case, to sustain them.

Sport allows the men the luxury of hope, which Yaz doesn't have. In a strange way, hope only comes to her in the aftermath of her horrific ordeal. If any change is to happen for her and for other women in her world, it will take a lone individual, a brave one to start that change – and Yaz, alone and scared but with the heart of a lioness, takes that first step towards hope and liberation.

PATRICIA LOGUE

Director / Cyfarwyddwr

SHERMAN THEATRE: CARDIFF'S AWARD-WINNING THEATRE
THEATR Y SHERMAN – THEATR WOBRWYOL CAERDYDD

Based in the heart of Cardiff, Sherman Theatre is a leading producing house with a particular focus on the development and production of new work.

Sherman Theatre makes and curates theatre for audiences in Wales, across the UK and internationally and develops the work of Welsh and Wales based artists.

The Sherman generates opportunities for the citizens of Cardiff to connect with theatre through inspiring and visionary engagement.

In 2018 Sherman Theatre became the first in Wales to win the Regional Theatre of the Year title at The Stage Awards, recognising the Sherman as the most exciting theatre in the UK, outside of London.

In April 2018, Sherman Theatre's production of *Killology* by Gary Owen and directed by former Artistic Director Rachel O'Riordan won the Olivier Award for Outstanding Achievement in Affiliate Theatre. This was a co-production with London's Royal Court Theatre.

Wedi'i lleoli yng nghanol Caerdydd, mae Theatr y Sherman yn dŷ cynhyrchu blaenllaw gyda ffocws benodol ar ddatblygu a chynhyrchu gwaith newydd.

Mae Theatr y Sherman yn creu a churadu theatr ar gyfer cynulleidfaoedd yng Nghymru, ar draws y DU ac yn rhyngwladol, ac yn datblygu gwaith artistiaid Cymreig a'r rheiny wedi'u lleoli yng Nghymru.

Mae'r Sherman yn creu cyfleoedd i drigolion Caerdydd fedru creu cyswllt â'r theatr trwy ymrwymiad ysbrydoledig a gweledigaethol.

Yn 2018 Theatr y Sherman fu'r cyntaf yng Nghymru i ennill teitl Theatr Ranbarthol y Flwyddyn yng Ngwobrau The Stage, gan gydnabod y Sherman fel y theatr mwyaf cyffrous yn y DU, tu hwnt i Lundain.

Ym mis Ebrill 2018, enillodd cynhyrchiad Theatr y Sherman o *Killology* gan Gary Owen ac wedi'i gyfarwyddo gan gyn-Gyfarwyddwr Artistig Rachel O'Riordan Gwobr Olivier am Lwyddiant Eithriadol mewn Theatr Gysylltiedig. Roedd *Killology* yn gyd-gynhyrchiad â'r Royal Court Theatre.

SHERMANTHEATRE.CO.UK   029 2064 6900 ◆◇◆

 Cyngor Celfyddydau Cymru
Arts Council of Wales
 Iechyd gan Lywodraeth Cymru
Noddwyd gan Lywodraeth Cymru
 Supported by The National Lottery® through the Arts Council of Wales
 Cefnogwyd gan Y Loteri Genedlaethol trwy Gyngor Celfyddydau Cymru

Sherman Cymru Productions Ltd | Registered Charity Number / Rhif Elusen Cofrestredig 1118364

SHERMAN THEATRE STAFF LIST
RHESTR STAFF THEATR Y SHERMAN

Executive Director / Cyfarwyddwr Gweithredol Julia Barry

Head of Finance and Administration / Pennaeth Cyllid a Gweinyddiaeth Sally Shepherd

Head of Marketing and Communications / Pennaeth Marchnata a Chyfathrebu Ed Newsome

Head of Production and Planning / Pennaeth Cynhyrchu a Chynllunio Mandy Ivory-Castile

Artistic Administrator & Executive Assistant / Gweinyddwr Artistig a Chynorthwy-ydd Gweithredol Corey Bullock

Bar & Kitchen Manager / Rheolwr y Bar a'r Gegin Jay Moore

Bar & Kitchen Supervisor / Goruchwyliwr y Bar a'r Gegin Kayleigh Edwards

Box Office Manager / Rheolwr y Swyddfa Docynnau Liz Thomas

Carpenter / Pensaer Mathew Thomas

Communities & Engagement Coordinator / Cydlynydd Cymundeau ac Ymgysylltu Timothy Howe

Company Stage Manager / Rheolwr Llwyfan y Cwmni Kevin Smith

Deputy House Manager / Dirprwy Reolwr Tŷ Keira Wilkie

Development Manager / Rheolwr Datblygu Michael Houghton

Finance Assistant / Cynorthwy-ydd Cyllid Julia Griffiths

House Manager / Rheolwr Tŷ Andrew Lovell

HR & Admin Assistant / Cynorthwy-ydd Gweinyddol ac Adnoddau Dynol Sophie Hughes

Marketing Manager / Rheolwr Marchnata Vanessa Williams

Marketing Officer / Swyddog Marchnata Rebecca Price

Multi Skilled Technician / Technegydd Aml-sgiliau Christiane Bérubé

Senior Electrician / Prif Drydanwr Rachel Mortimer

Sherman 5 Facilitator / Hwylusydd Sherman 5 Siân Mile

Sherman 5 Legacy Assistants / Cynorthwywyr Etifeddiaeth Sherman 5 Eileen Leahy & Lucy Purrington

Technical Stage Manager / Rheolwr Llwyfan Technegol Gareth Williams

Box Office Assistants / Cynorthwywyr Swyddfa Docynnau Ashley Roberts, Beshlie Thorp, Daisy Williams, Eileen Leahy, Elen Smith, Ellen Thomas, Ethan Jenkins, Holly Nesbitt, Kitty Hughes, Lily Greenslade-Davey, Non Haf Davies, Samantha Jones, Tom Blumberg

Café Bar team / Tim Bar Caffi Beshlie Thorp, CJ Rock, Dafydd Haine, Elisabeth Haljas, Iwan Hughes, Olivia Bolas, Rosie Rowell, Sam Jones

Thanks to our Front of House volunteers. Diolch i ein gwirfoddolwyr Blaen Tŷ.

BOARD OF TRUSTEES / YMDDIRIEDOLWYR

David Stacey (Chair / Cadeirydd)
Marlies Hoecherl
(Vice Chair / Is-gadeirydd)
Nicholas Carlton
Paul Clayton
Ceri Davies
Clive Flowers
Robert Keegan
Keith Morgan
Marc Simcox
Owen Thomas
Helen Vallis

DID YOU KNOW WE ARE A REGISTERED CHARITY? WE CAN ONLY DO WHAT WE DO THANKS TO YOUR SUPPORT.

A WYDDOCH CHI EIN BOD NI'N ELUSEN GOFRESTREDIG? FEDRWN NI OND GWNEUD YR HYN A WNAWN HEFO'CH CEFNOGAETH CHI.

As a registered charity, Sherman Theatre relies on support from individuals, companies, trusts and foundations to help us deliver our work both on and off stage.
Your support can ensure that the artistic success of the Sherman Theatre continues into the future.

Fel elusen gofrestredig, dibynna Theatr y Sherman ar gefnogaeth gan unigolion, cwmnïau, ymddiriedolaethau a sefydliadau er mwyn ein helpu i gyflawni ein gwaith ar y llwyfan ac oddi arni. Gall eich cymorth sicrhau fod llwyddiant artistig Theatr y Sherman yn parhau ymhell i'r dyfodol.

You can donate:

Online:
shermantheatre.co.uk/support-us

Gallwch wneud rhodd:

Ar-lein:
shermantheatre.co.uk/cefnogi

By phone:
please contact our Box Office team on 029 2064 6900

Dros y ffôn:
cysylltwch â thîm y Swyddfa Docynnau ar 029 2064 6900

If you would like to learn how you can support our work please contact:

Os hoffech ddysgu sut y gallwch gefnogi ein gwaith, cysylltwch â:

Michael Houghton
Development Manager / Rheolwr Datblygu
029 2064 6976 michael.houghton@shermantheatre.co.uk

LOSE YOURSELF

Katherine Chandler

Acknowledgements

Thanks to Patricia Logue, Aaron Anthony, Gabrielle Creevy and Tim Preston.

Also to Rachel O'Riordan, Sam John, Aled Pedrick, Laura Dingle, Connor Calland and Francesca Henry.

Guy O'Donnell and Mathonwy O'Donnell.

K.C.

For Mali

Characters

YAZ
JOSH
NATE

This text went to press before the end of rehearsals and so may differ slightly from the play as performed.

YAZ   When I first saw him, it snowed.
And it was the 2nd of May.
And it wasn't even Scotland.
And he's stood there in the snow.
Mr Snow.
And he's wearing this T-shirt that says:

She quotes the first five lines of 'Rapper's Delight' by The Sugarhill Gang,

Sugarhill Gang. 'Rapper's Delight'.

And he's looking at me as if to say, What the fuck? It's May?
And I'm looking back as if to say I know. It's May and it's snowing – The world's gone mental.
And I'm gonna say it,
I'm gonna go over to him and say it,
But then Samantha comes up to me all...
Yazmin Cole, it's raining, and you know what moisture does to my weave.
And when I look back to Mr Snow he's gone.

I think about him though.
Mr Snow.
He crosses my thoughts now and then
You know how sometimes they do.

JOSH   Here's the thing.
My anterior cruciate ligament split in three places and is currently being held together by a nail. Which, if I move my leg in a certain way, I can see protruding through my skin.
My skin. Intramedullary nail. Protrusion.
An alien invasion in my leg.
The nail holds the sections of bone together, it heals quicker that way. That's what they say.
A few years ago, that would have ended my career.

But now you have the nail in and you can pretty much
put weight on it straight away, because it's supporting
it, within the week you're putting weight through it.
By week six you're back on the turf.
The last break I had set me back a year, kept me down
in the leagues.
This might look like just another break to you.
A fracture. A pause in the progression of the
shooting star.
But for me it's life and death. That simple.
Life.
Death.
Cos if this don't heal right, and I can't play, I'm back
to one of three choices.
The dole, drugs or die young.
And I don't wanna die young.
Literally or metaphorically.
I wanna live forever.
S'why I chose football.
Not chose exactly.
It's in me.
Football chose me.
And here's the secret.
There is no secret.
You either got it or you haven't.
And I got it.
It's easy.
I don't even have to try.
And now. Now I'm a player.
It's like that with everything.
Well. Almost everything.

NATE   He's a strange little fucker.

JOSH   Bit harsh.

NATE   But I likes him. Taken him under my wing, haven't I?

JOSH   What he don't get is, I don't fit in and I likes it that way.
         I just wanna be left alone.
         For this break to heal and to get back to fitness, so
         I can end my season.

NATE   You'll be fine,
            I tells him this.

            I been telling him this since he done it.

            It's all part of it. I says. You'll be back on the turf
            before you know it.
            I've had hamstring strains, ankle sprains, split my tibia
            in two places AND
            ripped what cartilage I had left, outta both my knees.

JOSH   Course he has.

NATE   Once,
            I had a groin pull so bad my dick turned blue.
            I got photos if you want to see them?

JOSH   I don't.

NATE   Last year, I was out for three months, got a hernia,
            didn't I.
            Took on a life of its own, the lads called it Keith and
            painted it team colours, gave it a face.
            It was officially team mascot last October.
            I tell him this, thinking he might break a smile.

JOSH   I don't.

NATE   There's not one player in the leagues what haven't had
            time out through injury.
            You wait till you hit the championship or the premier,
            when they come at you...
            It's like being shelled by a battle tank.
            Then you'll know about injuries, is all I'm saying.

JOSH   I know about injuries.

NATE   He don't.
            I know.
            Cos I'm thirty-two.
            Not eighteen like him.
            Thirty-two. That's sixty-five in football years.
            My need to play is great but my body has other ideas.
            I'm at the end of my game.
            But Josh,
            Well

He's the rising star.
That's the way he likes it.
Man of the match.
Star of the season.
Player of the year.
You won't have heard of him.
Yet.
For now
But not for long,
He runs with me.
Down in the gutters, among the spit and the shit, the grassroots and the grizzle of League One.
Ascendant meets descendant in this part of the league,
And it ain't always clear which direction you're heading, especially after a messy Saturday.
Branded and Bespoke, Primark and Prada
Together as one.
Fleeting as fuck.

(*To* JOSH.) You need to get out of here.
Get yourself some action.

How long you been looking at these four walls with your mam for company?

JOSH   Fifty-seven days.

NATE   Right. Tonight's your lucky night, my boys are on their way down, you're about to have the night of your life.

JOSH   What about my leg?

NATE   I'll look after you mate. Leg included.

JOSH   I dunno, Nate.

NATE   It's hot out there man.
And the pussy.
The pussy is ripe.
And in this weather it's on show.
And we can use it to our advantage. This. The leg.
They're gonna love you.
With your disability.

I'll pick you up at eight.

JOSH   Nine?

NATE   Seven.

YAZ   The next time I see Mr Snow, is the day of my
         interview.
         I'm on the high street.
         This time it's June.
         And it's not snowing.

JOSH   Meg comes to see me.
         She always comes to see me after a shift.
         She's had a bitch of a day.
         As per.
         Meg's always had a bitch of a day.
         But to be fair she works in the drive-through
         McDonald's.
         So.
         Me and Meg had a thing.
         More than a thing.
         We got together in school.
         We had all the makings of Wayne and Coleen.
         Then I fucked it up.
         And without the Gucci handbags, Dubai holidays
         and twenty grand a week, my Coleen found it hard
         to forgive.
         There were texts on my phone, that she found.
         Moments of madness.
         It was only texts.
         But they were bad texts.
         I wouldn't hurt her.
         Didn't mean to.
         But the girls.
         You know.

         Meg's handing me a cuppa, black bag in hand, picking
         up wrappers and used tissues. She's telling me,
         People, are arseholes.
         Yep.
         I agree with everything Meg says.
         Cos this is what I have to do now.
         She holds the strings.
         What she says goes.

I'll get her back.
Because I want her back.
It's a matter of time.
A game of chess.
I try to hold her eye but she breaks it.
Sometimes, if the sun rises right and I catch her true,
she'll sit with me, close to me, play with my hands,
kiss my fingers.
She'll let me move on her.
Let me touch her.
Let me breathe her in.
But today she's giving me hate.
And I let her.
She knows I want her back.
So I let her.
Patience.
She wants me back.
I know she wants me back.
But she's saving face.
It's the game she plays.
I'll play her game.
Her beautiful game.

YAZ   Thank you for coming, Miss Cole, if you'd like to take
a seat.
The man tells me there's a scoring system.
A drop of sweat runs down my back.
Is there? I say, A scoring system. I see.
I have to score your answers.
He's sharp.
Nice one.
My voice don't sound like me.
I want this job.
That's all it is
Just a job
I wasn't cultivated for a career
I just want a job
He takes out a tissue and wipes his top lip, leaving
remnants of white fluff over his face.
He tells me whoever scores the highest, goes through
to the next round.

There's a next round? I say.

I'm aware that Samantha's waiting for me outside
Greggs and she only has an hour.

And nobody said nothing about rounds.

I thought I'd be in and out.

A chat, they said.

He clicks the top of his pen and writes something on
a form. There's three.

Three?

Like *X Factor* or something.

I laugh. Too loud. Too big.

For fuck's sake.

Why am I still laughing?

He glares at me from over the top of his glasses.

I'm fucking it up.

And I really want this job.

I need to save my arse. Ask something good.

Something that makes sense.

Can I just ask, this is for the make-up counter?

He sneezes.

Are you telling me you don't know what job you've
applied for?

No. I know. I just. I wanted to ask something. I…

Stop talking Yaz.

I just…

Beg. Try begging.

Look. Please. Um sir. I just wanted to say how much
I really want this.

His disinterest is tangible.

Too much? Not enough? Who knows. I go in hard.

I did a beauty course? Level 2, NVQ in beauty and nail
services? Will that score?

Fuck it. Shit or bust.

I got a paper. A… one of them… it's square. What's
it called. A certificate. With NVQ on it… you know
the ones?

A certificate?

Yeah. That's it. A certificate. Level 2.

Nailed it, Yaz.

He tells me they got girls with degrees lining up for
this job.

Rats racing to get in the rat pack.
In what? In make-up?
They do degrees in standing all day at a make-up
counter?
He looks to the floor. Can't look me in the eye.
That come out wrong.
Bollocks.
He reshuffles his papers.
This is well and truly blown.
He pulls the tissue back out of his pocket, blows
his nose.
Shall we get started?

NATE   After training, I'm in Al's café.
All-day breakfast.
A few heads turn.
Course they do.
I'm a good-looking fella and the locals know me.
Round here I'm Giggsy, Ronaldo and Kane.
Who's not gonna want a second look.
I order the works.
The full English, double egg, bacon and sausage, black
pudding, yes please, easy on the beans, no fried bread.
Sure?
No fried bread.
Tea. Strong and sweet.
That'll set me up.
For tonight.
Here he isn't, the big star, fucking Malaka.
Al the Greek.
As Cardiff as they come.
Whatsa matter with my fried bread now?
I wanna make it to forty.
You saying my fried bread not good enough now, not
good enough for the big striker eh?
Behind him on the shelf with the ketchup and the
cooking oil is a blown-up photo of me and him, from
my first match for the Ravens last season.
He's wearing the shirt I gave him and a club scarf.
Pride of place.
There's two types of fans.

The ones that wants to talk about football and the ones
that wants to talk about your money.
With Al it's always the football.
And the women.
He likes to hear about the women.
You getting plenty, striker boy? He slaps a tea towel
over his shoulder and leans in to the counter.
Does Dolly Parton sleep on her back?
He likes that, mimes me a Parton chest, laughs again as
he pours me my tea.
Bet the poor fucker can't get it up no more.

JOSH I've dozed off and when I come to, Meg has gone and
my Auntie San is hiking up my good leg and hoovering
under it.
Behind her my mam is smoking a fag, all rolling eyes
and steaming sighs.
Generally Auntie San don't stay long.
Thank fuck.
It's uncomfortable for everyone.
My mam don't know why she still comes.
I do.
The exquisite pleasure of knowing she's better than us.
But it won't be that way for long.
Football's my ticket outta here.
The great escape.
Is that how you're going? San says, Like that?
What? I says, knowing how I look but who gives
a shit when I'm sat in the house.
Would it kill you to run a brush through your hair?
Heard of soap have you?
Your Uncle Lee is outside in the car. He's had time off
to fetch you up and you can't even be arsed to wash?
Fetch me up where? I says.
The hospital Joshie boy. Your appointment? Was it
your leg got broke or your head?
She ruffles my hair like I'm still a kid and for a second I
think about telling her to fuck off out of here. But I don't.
She's been good to us over the years so I don't.
Looked after me a few times when things got a bit
tight for my mum.

I pulls myself up and looks out the window.
There he is.
Sat there, strumming his fingers on the steering wheel
to whatever easy-listening shite is on the radio.
This is the highlight of his week, the sad git.
Leader of the 'live slow, die old' brigade.
He's been sixty since his twenties.
You got ten minutes so get your arse in gear.
Auntie San slaps my arse with a tea towel.
She thinks it's funny.
I heads to the bathroom and turns the taps on full steam.

NATE   I sit in my usual seat by the window.
Sign a club programme for a kid who's in a Man U
away strip, cheeky fucker.
But he's come over with his ma so.
I take the piss out of his shirt and find the page in the
programme that shows me shooting for goal.
His ma's purposely dropped her pen so she can bend
over right in front of my face.
I help her pick it up, give her arse a rub as I reach
past her.
Hold it there a bit.
One good turn deserves another.
Nice arse.
I sit back.
Signs the page. Fake-punch the kid in the arm. Ruffle
his hair.
His ma's playing it cool.
Nice tits.
Nicer with my face in them.
The kid's run back to what looks like his nana,
showing her the page.
Ma's asking me for her pen back.
I hold it in my hand.
Offer it to her.
She goes to take it but I hold on to it. For a second.
She tugs it.
I'm playing with her.
She knows it.
She tugs again.

With attitude.
Which I like.
Don't want it given up too easy.
She pulls it outta my hand.
Rips a bit of skin off my thumb as she pulls.
Bit fierce.
Walking away she puts the pen in her arse pocket and
I know she can't quite believe her luck.
I've made her day.
She sits facing me. Can't take her eyes off. Yeah, you
wanna piece of this don't ya, darling.
Well, keep looking.
Maybe one day.
Still the attitude, all pouty. You never know your luck,
sweetheart.
She's getting up.
Course she is.
Nan's fussing the kid to put his coat on.
The kid runs for the door with Nana in hot pursuit.
Ma holds back.
Course she does.
Puts on her jacket – bit plastic but
Hang onto your horses, here she comes.

You ever touch me again and I'll have you for assault.
Hear me?
I look around.
Me?
Assault – when? What?
The arse-rub?
Is that what you mean?
Are you fucking kidding me?
Assault?
You hear me?

I'll give you assault.
Have you seen my thumb? I'll need a plaster on that.

Do.
You.
Hear.
Me?

I hear you.

She slams out of the café, muttering Pervert as
she goes.
Time of the month, no doubt.
Feminist.
Feminazi.
I know what she needs.
Jesus.
What has the world fucking come to.

YAZ   Samantha's sat on the bench eating a steak bake and
a sausage roll.
She takes a look at my face, taps the bench next to her.
It's a shit job anyway,
I slump down.
I heard they're just taking on people to cover the
summer and come September they'll dump them saying
profits are down. You're better off in the nail bar.
She smiles and tucks my hair behind my ear.
Loops her arm through mine.
I wanted it.
I thought I could, you know, move up when I learned
the ropes. I thought it had more going for it.
Opportunities. I don't wanna work in the nail bar for
the rest of my life,
what the fuck am I gonna do now.
She offers me the last bite of her bake.
And we sit for a bit.
Not saying what we both know to be true.
This is it.
This is it for us.
Shit jobs
In shit towns.
Shit lives.
The liberation might have happened to you
The preachers, the converted,
but for us
for the many not the few
It's not true
It never cared about us

It never even knew us.
The liberators never even looked.

So we sit
for a bit.

Then Samantha says.
I know what'll cheer you up.
What? I say.
We're going out. Tonight.
I'm not going anywhere.
Two words. Josh. Taylor.
Who?
Only JOSH TAYLOR! Ravens? Is only who.
The arse on him. I'd ruin him.
She would an' all.
I don't know who you're talking about? I say.
Striker for the Ravens?
He's their biggest talent. He's had a couple of injuries
that set him back but he's going places, Yaz. Like BIG.
TIME.
And
She shakes her head like she can't even believe it.
He's hung like a donkey.
Oh him…
I got who he is.
They're out tonight. They'll be at Extreme.
How d'you know?
I have my ways
She jabs at my sides, throws back her head and laughs.
She's on a mission.
She tickles me.
Josh Taylor though.
Even though she's a feminist, she does favour a big dick.
She tickles me again.
Makes me laugh.
FUCK IT!
She screams at the top of her voice to FUCK THE
JOB.
FUCK THEM ALL.
This is the real world

Her and she and me. We.
We gotta do, what we gotta do
Like we always did
So Fuck you
And you
And you
Her and me.
Yeah.
Today is all we got.
Now.
Right now.
Alive in the moment.
One life
So let's live it, let's grab it
and fuck them all.

JOSH   There's good news and there's bad.
I says tell me the bad please doc, cos bad was not
a word I was expecting so I wants to get it done.
He starts with the good.
He says the wound is healing nicely.
Better than he'd imagined.
And the bones are fixing in the way he would hope for
a man of my age and fitness level.
So that's all good that, he says.
He waits for me to agree.
My Auntie San nods.
There we go, she says, he haven't cracked a smile in
over a month, he's delighted, look at his face.
Tell me the bad, I says.
It's the nerves. He says.
With the substantial break we expected a period of
numbness and swelling but
BUT
The prolonged period of numbness you've experienced
in your foot, would suggest there's more of a problem
than we first imagined.
To add to that the bone is fixing well but it's slightly
off-course.
His mouth is moving and talking, but I'm lost in the
names of bones and nerves and fractures that sound

like a foreign language to me.
I'm a footballer, I says.
Yes, he agrees but he's not listening.
I play football. I say.
Yes, he says again but he don't hear.
See the thing is, San says, is he's worried about his
football.
His football.
She says it like it's the least of my worries
But it's the only worry.
I got nothing else.

Am I getting better?
He's pointing at shady slides of patellas and femurs,
fibulas and tibias.
Creating angles with his arms, expressive as he talks.
Tell me I'm getting better.
Auntie San's a nodding dog, appeasing him, clueless.

Is this getting better?
Am I getting the fuck better?

I see from their faces I've said it out loud.
He's been a bit down with it all, San says, excusing
my behaviour.

We would strongly advise you considering a rebreak
and reset.
A what? I says, A fucking what?
It's a simple enough procedure.

But it's better, I feel that it's better.
I stand up.
I thought you'd be getting the cast off, that's what
I thought.
I'm pointing to the leg like he don't understand that it's
my leg we're all talking about.
You said it was better.
That's what you said last time.
He's picking up his papers, shuffling them, puts them
under his arm.
We were optimistic is, I think, what I said. He nods at
my Auntie San as he starts for the door.

This is all he's gonna give me.
Mate, I'm in his way, in his face. My Auntie San
stands and puts her hand on my arm.
It's taking everything I got, not to do something really
stupid, like punch him in the face.
Mate, I says, You don't understand. I gotta be back
before the end of the season. You don't understand.
He moves past me.
Mister. Doctor. They'll write me off. I'll be wasted.
Me. I'll be waste.
His hands on the door,
We appreciate it's the very last thing you want, but
long-term, it really is the best way forward.
It's slipping away.
Down the plughole.
Waste.
The dole, drugs or die young.
There's no plan B.

NATE   Three o'clock and I'm up the high street.

YAZ   I got nothing to wear.
So now I got to find something that makes me look
half-decent.
Because next to Samantha.
I'm just cellophane.
We start to walk back to the boutique where Samantha
works.

NATE   I'm in the One Stop.
Getting flowers.

YAZ   And that's when I see him again.
In the window of the one stop.
Him, you know
Mr Snow.

NATE   Now, I'm no Gok Wan but even I knows this shit
display of primary-coloured chrysanths wrapped in
plastic ain't gonna cut it.

YAZ   Mr hip hop, hippie to the hippie... You know how it
goes.

NATE   The mags by the till catch my eye and I get to
       wondering if they still stock a full top shelf.
       Course they do.

YAZ   His hair is beautiful.
       Jeans and a tee.

NATE   I go to pay.

YAZ   He walks towards me.

NATE   At the window, there's a girl pressed against the glass
       looking right at me.
       Part of the job.

YAZ   He winks.

NATE   I wave.
       Polite like.

YAZ   I just stand there.

NATE   Run along, there's a good girl.

YAZ   I think I'm smiling.

NATE   Her mate joins the party at the window.

YAZ   I look into his eyes, he holds my look.
       And I get a jolt of – what is that – something –
       electricity – I know, like cringe – but it is.
       He waves.

NATE   I wave and wink back.
       She's a bit cheap but cute.
       With less make-up she might be beautiful.

YAZ   He's beautiful.
       He reaches into his pocket and grabs a handful of
       change.
       The muscles on his arms flex.

NATE   Her tits are pressing up against the shop window.

YAZ   His T-shirt sits tight and I can make out the shape of
       his pecs.

NATE   The swell of her thighs.

YAZ   The line of his legs.

NATE   I like how she looks.

YAZ   I like how he looks.

        Pause.

        Don't fucking look now
        Samantha.

NATE   The other one's all blonde and big balls.
        There's hundreds like her.
        Mass-produced.
        I know how she tastes.

YAZ   She's grabbed my arm like a vice.
        Nate West is waving at me.
        Who? I says.
        Nate West is only who. Ravens' new striker is
        only who.
        I look around.
        Where? I can't see anyone.
        I look at Samantha.
        Follow her gaze.
        Follow it through the glass.
        Follow it to Mr Snow.
        She waves back.
        At my Mr Snow.
        He puts his hand down.
        Nate West? I say. Rudry Town?
        His dick's been to places other dicks don't dare
        to tread.
        Even so. She fusses her hair.
        I take a step away from Samantha and turn back to
        Mr Snow.
        I smile.
        He winks again.
        At me.
        Definitely me.
        Nate West winked at me.
        And then he's gone.
        I don't look at Samantha but she's stopped talking.

And I know she's all rattled cos she thinks it's all
about her.
It is always about her.
But not this time.

JOSH   Text. Meg. Emoji. Four-leaf clover. Horseshoe.
WhatsApp, night-out group. Nate. Picture of a potato
that looks like an arse.
Text. My mam. Can I lend her a twenty.
Hospital appointment was a fuck-up Mam, thanks
for asking.
WhatsApp. Nate. Picture of a girl in a nightclub
sucking a dick, being sprayed with champagne.
Nate. US. TONIGHT. In caps.
Classic Nate.
Text. Meg. Smiley face emoji.
Text. My mam. Telling me not to be a dickhead.
WhatsApp. Nate. Picture. Hotel room. Titwank.
Text. My mam. And a tenner would do it, if I get her
a packet of fags on the way home.
WhatsApp. Nate. Question. A blowjob or a titwank?
Pros and Cons. Discuss.
Text. From Meg. How'd it go? Thumbs-up. Question
mark.

I turn off my phone and tells my Uncle Lee to pull over
by the shop on the corner so I can get my mum fags.
I'll wait by here, he says, keeping the engine running.
Nah, cheers but you get off. I taps the roof of his
estate, I'm good from here.
We'll wait, Auntie San's winding down the window to
cut me a look.
I say, Auntie San, I can walk up the street without
a babysitter, the very same street I been walking up for
eighteen years unaccompanied. Now, if you'd be so
kind as to piss off and let me get about my day.
We battle it out, eye to eye, stare to stare and for once
Uncle Lee finds his bollocks, puts her window up and
slowly pulls away.
Round the corner, behind the shop is where I used to
kick a ball around when I was a kid. I was allowed to

the shop and around but I weren't allowed further on
past the stream.
When we was in Year 10 me and Meg used to bunk off
and go to the stream.
She'd have me making wishes and holding my breath,
throwing sticks and shit with notes tied on, carving our
names in the trees and all that stuff.
All the time I'd be trying it.
Cos there was never anyone else in my head.
Never anyone I wanted like her.
I wait on the bridge for a bit looking into the stream
and then crosses over it and into the wreck. There's
a group of kids playing footie on the five-a-side pitch.
I'd take a ball there any time of day and night and play
on my own. In games I'd score eight, ten goals on
that pitch.
The smell of the field takes me right back and fills me
with all the reasons why I play the game. All the
possibilities that football opens up to a kid like me.
Football is my chance. My escape.
I have to fight through.

YAZ   I end up with a top from the boutique.
It's nice.
Fuck that, it's like amazing.
It's not see-through but you can see enough, so.
Bosh.
With a sexy little knicker skimmer.
Double bosh.
Mr Snow and a fuck-off top in one day.
Come on.
There'll be other jobs.
Double come on.
And
Things happen in threes.
So in my book that means tonight's going to be
a show-stopper.
And that'll make the three.
Cos me and Sam, when we gets it on us,
me and her are firecrackers. Light us and watch us roar.
Lock up your sons.

And your daughters if the mood fits.
Tonight we are getting destroyed.

NATE   Text from the wife.
Get milk and bread. Not home till after eight, Lydia's
got ballet.
Result.
She won't be home.
Text. The wife.
And nappies.
I love her, my wife, but she's zero to a hundred in
a second and before we know where we are we're
taking chunks out of each other.
And tonight I'm after an energy release of an
altogether different kind.
And another text.
DON'T FORGET (capitals) to stop in the post office
for a passport form.
Dubai.
Two weeks.
Can't wait.
Gotta make the most of it cos at my age you're never
guaranteed your next game let alone your next season
and now I'm on loan, the rope is fraying fast.
Text. The wife. Again. You gotta be kidding me.
LOVE YOU. Capitals. Heart emoji.

YAZ   Back at mine.
It's gone seven.
Samantha says the top don't look right cos it's funny
on my tits.
It's a shame you got no arse, she says, which might
have – might have – compensated for your funny tits in
a Kim Kardashian sort of way.
She shakes her head, baffled by the shape of me.
We'll just have to try and make the best of the tit
situation with a better bra.
I'm not wearing a bra, I tells her.
Makes sense, she says.
She knows a trick that involves sellotape and cling film
that could get me out of a situation here.

She gets to work.
Multitasking
Make-up and pre-drinks.
Loosen us up. Get the juices flowing.
The skill here is beginning the drinking early enough
to dull the senses
and free up the creativity but without peaking too early
and ending up looking like the joker, face down in a
toilet bowl before you've even set foot in a taxi
marked 'good times'.
We've got Cava
Aldi, four ninety-nine
and my stupid brother turns up with half a bottle of
voddy. Punch. It all goes in together.
I'm hot.
I'm looking cream.
I'm looking double cream, extra thick.
I'm on fucking fire.

JOSH   How'd it go?
I should tell Meg what the hospital said. She'd tell me
it'll all be fine. We'll get through it.
But I'm a knob so I don't.

I text her back.
Come round tonight.
She's straight back at me.
No can do, soz.
Night out with the girls.
Winking emoji.

YAZ   Tony turns up.
He couldn't look any more like a taxi driver if he tried.
Always on time.
Always got something around his mouth.
Generally curry, ketchup or custard. Occasionally
crumbs. Occasionally all of the above.
I try not to look.
But I want to know if – yes – ketchup.
Ladies.
Tony.
Always the same banter.

Your chariot awaits.

Yeah.

Out tonight in search of your princes, is it?

You got it.

To take you away from all of this.

Always.

If I was ten years younger...

Ten?

Twenty then.

We'll let you have that.

If I was twenty years younger...

You'd still be twenty years too old.

Always in red and black.

Big fan of the Ravens.

Always in his cab.

Never seen his legs.

My brother Darren has. Once. In a charity night up the snooker club.

Never heard of coats, you two. You'll catch your death.

Every time.

I like his face. I think it's kind.

Samantha reckons he might have been good looking before he got fat.

Turn it up, Tone.

Tony likes Lionel Richie. And the Commodores.

Which is not the same thing apparently.

Will you need me later?

We'll call you, Tone.

Don't let anyone buy you drinks and always take your drinks to the loo with you.

Jesus.

Energy drain.

And stay together. Look out for each other.

Double Jesus.

Life on the edge.

Always the same.

NATE   Seven o'clock and I'm outside Joshie's in a cab.
The guns are out and even if I say so myself, I'm packing it.
By seven-thirty, we're in the beer garden of The Coach.

I gets Josh settled on a bench, where he can stretch out
his leg.
Outta sight of the pissheads that are larging it.
One sniff that the Ravens are around and we're easy
target.
Pint and a chaser, while we wait for the crew.
As a general rule, when your face is known, it's best to
get your core squad out with you from the get-go.
They're not all players, just a few, I'm not a fucking
idiot.
I need back up for when it gets a bit messy, which it
does, every time. Some little dickhead off his face who
fancies his chances, and decides to take against my
score sheet of late.
Step forward Solo and Dano.
Text – Solo – they've checked into the hotel and on
their way.
They got a spare room.
We'll make use of that later, I tells Joshie.
He knows the score.
And he finally lifts his head from his phone.
This lot and their phones.
Text – The wife. Flowers and a heart.
For fuck's sake.

JOSH   Nate's out to get laid.

NATE   These days, the young pros, they don't know how
          to live.

JOSH   So that's a bad start.

NATE   The parties we used to have.
          In the championship anything and everything goes,
          with anyone.
          We was Roman emperors.
          This lot though.
          They need to let loose.

JOSH   My need to escape this is as pressing as Nate's need to
          fuck as many women as possible.

NATE   Tame.
          Lame.

JOSH   I might head off.

NATE   He'll learn. Cos I'll teach him.
         You're going nowhere.

JOSH   Seriously. My head's not in it Nate.
         Mate.
         I'll get an Uber.

NATE   Sit there. What you having?
         I'll see you right.

JOSH   I'm not right. That's the thing. I'm not right. It's the
         leg. You know.

NATE   Don't be a pussy. What you having?

JOSH   Nate stands tall at the bar.
         Nods his head over to the barman and a sea of people
         part for him, bypassing hands waving with attention-
         seeking notes.
         Guys high-five him, for his championship years.
         Heads tip themselves to him.
         Last week he played so
         This week he gets respect.
         When things go well he's the hero.
         They go wrong and he's the patsy, the punchbag
         The scapegoat they need to escape the drear of
         their lives.

NATE   I'm negotiating my way back to Joshie with a handful
         of lagers and a packet of cheese and onion hanging
         from my mouth.
         Some kids make a beeline.
         Back-slaps and head-rubs.
         How long till you're drawing your pension? A kid with
         no chins playing the joker.
         Alright lads.
         Backlash, the boozed-up bravados, goading for a fight,
         after a season of discontent.
         Didn't you used to play? His mate's joined the party.
         I could chew him up, spit him out.
         They roll him out once a season, oil his joints.
         They're pissing themselves.

Little rats, spending their days with their dicks in their
hands wishing there was something more to life.
No-Chin puts a finger on my chest.
And pushes.

JOSH   A commotion stirs in the middle of the pub.
The smash of glass.
The splash and spray of warm lager reaches my leg.
Dano and Solo materialise
from nowhere,
leapfrogs the benches like they found superpowers in
the bottom of their pint glasses. Swatting away any
trouble.
In the centre of the commotion they lift a grinning
Nate like a trophy, place him on their shoulders.
Nate fists the air like a warrior, baited by the crowd,
chanting his name.

YAZ   Me and Samantha hits the town.
Look out.
We skip the queue outside Extreme.
Dave the Door.
Samantha and him got history.
Which is handy.
Cos it means we skip the queue AND we gets into the
VIP's
AND
We never pays for nothing.
Tonight it's mental and Dave is distracted with a
lightweight who's curled up on the floor dribbling and
crying to the rest of her group, about how she 'always
ruins everything'.
She's holding Dave's ankle and begging him to
'give her five minutes and a pint of water and she'll
be fine'.
Classy.
She's on her back now, on the pavement, legs bending
and sprawling in ways that are only achievable by the
pissed.
Rolling and wailing in the gutter among the chips and
piss of the night and I'm exposed to more of her than
I care for.

Her tit has made an appearance and I can see she's
gone retro down below.

Her bush, fuzzy and damp and brown is curling around
the triangle of her knickers.

Gross.

Samantha reckons it's the new black.

She tried it once when she was seeing Lewis Bird.

Never again she says.

The stink.

Lewis fucking loved it though.

Couldn't leave it alone.

Dirty bastard.

And Dave's enjoying his bird's-eye view.

He winks at Samantha and nods us in.

She rubs his arse.

Are we still on your tab?

Dave nods.

Be careful up there, he shouts after us, the Ravens are
in tonight and they ain't taking any prisoners.

We climb the stairs to the inner door.

That means Josh Taylor.

Samantha squeals so high I'm worried for the glass in
the vicinity.

The door swings open and the heat and swell and base
and thump encases us and pulls us in.

NATE   By eleven we're in Extreme.

The place is shady and the smell of game is in the air.

The music rattles the floor.

I sit Josh on a stool in the VIP out of the crowd, next to
a group of girls, one of thems crying and dribbling to
her friend who's rapping along to the club tune but
don't actually know the words.

Take a peek at yourself, love. This ain't 'Carpool
Karaoke'.

Maybe that's why your mate's crying.

Having to sit there with James Corden.

How the fuck they made it into the VIP's is beyond me.

The state of them.

All plastic shoes and Rimmel London.

Offensive to the senses.

JOSH   Hell is other people.

YAZ   Vodka and Coke.
        Two.
        Down, down.
        Vodka and Coke.
        Two.
        Doubles.
        Bang, bang.
        Banging bass.
        Is it?
        Don't say it Yaz.
        I'm saying it Samantha.
        Is it though?
        Time!
        We slams our empty glasses down.
        Tequila.
        Shot.
        One.
        Two.
        Keeping it down.
        Just.
        And another for luck.
        I always said good things comes in threes.
        Three.
        We move to the crush of the dance floor and it's all
        hips and tits, flesh and brawn.

JOSH   Dano takes it upon himself to look out for me.
        He tells me and the group of girls, in detail about
        a recent cancer scare his father's prostate had, which,
        although interesting, wasn't conclusive to a banging
        atmosphere.
        His hand's on a girl's thigh as he speaks.
        The girl falls asleep.
        Dano sees this as an opportunity and lifts her skirt.
        Mate, I says and grabs his hand, come on.
        What? His hand goes higher. He's grinning.
        Don't.
        Still grinning he upskirts her.
        I knock the phone off his hand.
        Delete it.

Dano laughs, tells me I'm a boring cunt, winks.
As he deletes he tells me there's only one reason
people comes to this nightclub, the girls in the VIP's
know what they're here for.
I take his phone to see it's gone.
To be honest, I don't have a fucking thing to say to the
guy so I'm grateful when the DJ unleashes Beyoncé.
There's all sorts of squealing and jumping.
There's nasty shrieky singing.
And there's shit twerking happening – mostly from
Dan.
But luckily there's sambucca
One shot, two shot
And *Super Mario 3*.

NATE   I squeeze through sweaty bodies all rocking and
moving as one, the DJ shouts out for noise from
'everyone who's looking to get laid', everyone shouts
back, together united, like the home stand on match
day, rising and falling, the damned united.
I hold my beer high, dance my way through the sway
to the bar.
Solo passes back bottles and lines up the sambuccas.
Course he does.
The bar manager sets us up with a platter of shots in
the VIP's
Pace yourself Nate
Too late
Me and the boys demolish them.
The birds are flocking.
Course they are.
The hunt for cunt has begun and I'm in the thick of it,
cutting a naughty one on the dance floor.
And they're all, Go Nate, giggling and wiggling, and
I'm grinding an' winding.
Tits and arse, out to play.
Let me help you with those my darling.
Grounding and pounding.
I'm surrounded.
The hips are out.
I can't believe you can do that, Nate.

Jesus.
This is too easy.
I could have any one of them.
Should see what I can do with these in the bedroom,
babes.
These hips pull birds.
Fact.
These hips are fucking electric.
What I can't do with these hips, ain't worth doing, no
it ain't.
Josh over there, he gives it face.
Sits there, silent, staring.
The booze is fixing me right
I give it hips.
In my head I'm the perfect blend of Pharrell and Justin
Timberlake.
A dancers' smoothie.
I'm as cool as a cucumber.
As bendy as Beckham.
There's two types of people in this world, them what
make things happen and them what watch things happen.
Know who you are.
Tonight.
I know who I am.
I'm Nate fucking West.
Look at me.
Nathaniel James West.
And every fucker in here wants to have me.

YAZ   Me and Samantha turns it on.
It's a well-practised routine.
She winks at me.
Licks her lips.
Bumping and grinding.
She's kissing me.
Fuck it.
I'm kissing her back.
Rubbing and writhing.
They're loving it.
Loving us.
Letting it all go.

I am woman.
Watch me roar.

JOSH   According to Dano I'm a cockblocker.
Tells me to shape up.
Informs me that the general philosophy of the Ravens'
night out is that anything goes.
And I'm supposed to go with anything.
They do.
I've seen them.
Been with them when they hook the slutty brigade.
Watched it happen.
The promoters promote their goods.
The girls are shipped into the club, willing participants.
Dressed for success.
Hunting for a meal ticket.
Stories to sell and tell.
The lads ready to come and run.
I know them
I see them
Become-a-wag-dot-com
How-to-marry-a-footballer-dot-co-dot-uk
But it's not for me.
I'm no one's badge of honour.

YAZ   Tequila!
No more.
One more.
No more now.
And again.
Not again.
You got me.
Samantha is eating the face off some guy at the bar.
NOT Josh Taylor,
Not for the want of trying
It's Luke Fisher. Defender.
Surprise of the century.
He's fit.
She's been there done that
More than once.
Not full sex.

Cos he's a filthy pig with an unhealthy interest in
shop mannequins
She knows. She's been to his flat.

I scan the joint.

Swirling and swaying.
Then I sees it.
In all its glory, throbbing, eagerly calling me to it.
An empty chair.
A vision in maroon-crushed velour.
Like gold dust.
There's a route that's gonna take me swiftly to the
chair but it's gonna involve a series of moves requiring
skill and care to curveball the crush of the thumping
dance floor.
But my feet have stopped working properly in these
fucking shoes.

NATE   In the VIP Joshie's a sitting target.
This kid is a pussy magnet.
If only he knew it.
Solo's technique is to look like he don't give a shit,
he's the king of the 'treat 'em mean, keep 'em keen'
brigade.
Fair play.
It works for him.
And Dano is more of a befriender, then break-them-
down-over-time type of guy.
But this kid.
I've studied his technique and from what I've seen it
looks like he ain't got one.
And I don't think you can count 'stand and stare' as
a technique exactly. He don't even have to try. He's
either not interested or not interested is his technique.
Either way it works.
They love him.
The girls next to him are in chatter overdrive and he's
in fucking hell.
Now they're both singing.
He's smiling through it.
Good lad.

YAZ   I kick off my shoes and decide to go the long way
        round to the chair which is a risky choice I know but
        any one of these other fuckers could make it there
        before me.
        At the very least the scenic route allows me a safe
        passage over, clinging to the sweating and sticky walls
        and floors.
        Yaz.
        My brother.
        What the fuck.
        Where is she? He says.
        Sweating and grey.
        Eyes hollowed.
        Tapping to a different beat.
        The smell of him is making me nauseous.
        Go home, Darren.
        Where is she?
        He means Samantha
        He's been sniffing around of late
        Stop acting like a fucking psycho sex offender.

        Across the floor, my chair pulses in the throbbing light,
        calling me to it.

        You're a bitch.
        Like a fly on shit.
        I can't get rid
        Fuck off, Darren, you junkie.
        I push him out of my way.
        Bodies are doubling and the air is thickening.
        The swell at the bar is six-deep.
        Samantha is buried and obscured.
        I find my way to the chair.
        And – miracle of fucking miracles – there's no one sat
        on it.
        I sink into it and rub my feet.
        And if the world would just do me the favour of not
        spinning for five seconds then I can get back to my night.
        I sit.
        Close my eyes.
        The bump and the bass and the voices and the squeals

and the laughter, all the sounds of the night, all blend
into a muggy dull hub.
And I sit.
And breathe.
And again.
In and out.
And the world stops spinning.
Result.

NATE   Josh hits another sambucca as the merry-go-round of
pussy takes a fresh spin.
Baiting the king of cool.
A new piece sinks into the chair next to him, shoes in
hand, rubbing her feet.
I know her.
I recognise her tits.
It's the chick in the window of the One Stop.
My dick responds accordingly.
I grab a bottle of complimentary fizz.
She's about to find out that tonight's her lucky night.

YAZ   I open my eyes.
And he's there.
Mr Snow.
Stood right in front of me.
And I don't know if it's real so I close them again.
And breathe.
And I open my eyes.
Slowly.
Blink a bit.
Rub them clear.
Focus.
He's there.
Blazer
Velvet
No socks
Mr Snow.
And this time he's smiling.
And I'm smiling back.

JOSH   The swarm on the dance floor move as one.
A murmuration.

Guys in their freshest threads, girls garnished and gilded.
The hunt and the hunted.
Swooping and shifting.
Sucked into the music and movement, tribal and
unified.
Then I see her.
Meg.
My Meg.
A sharp jolt in my gut.
Her hair is different.
Done.
She looks done.
And her face.
She's all attitude.
Swagger and sway.
Her head shifting this way and that, on beat, always
on beat.
Behind her, this mug.
The jolt moves to my heart.
His hands are on her.
Bad move, mate.
She'll have you now, stupid fuck.
I wait.
She doesn't.
His hands are still there.
She smiles.
Grinds close.
Puts her hands on his hands.
Closer.
He lifts her hair.
Whispers something in her ear.
She laughs.
Puts her arms around his neck.
She laughs.
He touches her face.
She laughs.
And again.
Throws back her head and laughs.
And I thinks to myself that nothing is that funny from
where I'm standing.

NATE   I lead the One Stop chick to the VIP bathroom.
        Shake up the champagne.
        The fizz explodes spraying us both. She giggles.
        Nose wrinkles.
        I like her.
        She grabs the bottle. Sucks on the end of it.
        I like her even more.
        Gulps down the fizzing liquid. Licks the bottle end.
        Lets it spill down her mouth, her chin, her neck.
        My turn.
        I lick the spill that's running down her neck,
        Between her tits.
        She gasps.
        Giggles.
        She searches for my chin and pulls my head to her face.
        Wet and hungry.
        Bubbles of champagne still fizz around her mouth.
        I think about that fizz on my dick.
        What that fizz would do to her pussy.
        I swig the bottle of champagne
        Gulp it down.
        Put the bottle to her mouth
        She swigs it
        Puts the bottle on the floor
        I kiss her
        She kisses me back
        Hard.
        I lift up her skirt.
        Slip my fingers into her pants
        Her hands are on me
        Moving over me
        Pulling me
        Mr Snow
        If you like, darling.
        My fingers find their way to her
        She pushes against them
        Moans
        Mr Snow
        I drop down.
        Swig from the bottle again.

My tongue, still fizzing, gets to work on making
her come
She does
Course she does
I stand
Undo my trousers
She giggles.
Come-drunk.
Mr Snow
If you like, I say,
I like, she giggles.
She drops down.
Looks up at me
Eyes wide open
And swigs the bottle again.

JOSH   I need to go.
I stand and look across the club for Nate.
He's coming out of the bog with a slutty type hanging
on his back.
Standard night out for Nate
That bog should have his name on the door
I gotta get out of here.
Mate
Nate
I gotta get out of here.

NATE   Outside, the fresh air hits us
She sits on the floor.
Her top is pulled up and reveals her tummy.
Rolls of soft white flesh.
Even after two kids my missus is all skin and bone,
starved like a gypsy's dog.
I like them full.
Round.
I like them with the putty.
Soft and warm.
Secrets.
Hidden
In the folds and untolds.
Secrets shared with a kiss or a lick.

Not wound and tight
Not bones at night.
The putty tells me she don't take herself too seriously.
Tells me we can have a laugh.
Tells me she like the good things.
She looks at me and giggles.
Her freckles are cute.
She's got something about her.
I kneel down to her.

YAZ   Mr Snow is with me.
        Here.
        With me.
        Mr fucking Snow.
        I can't believe my luck.

NATE   Hello Freckles.
        I sit next to her on the floor and she puts her head on
        my shoulder.
        She reaches for my hand.
        Turns it over.
        Runs her fingers over my palm.
        Says something about snowing in Scotland.
        Puts her hand in mine.
        I weave my fingers through hers
        And hold
        I hold.

JOSH   Why is she still fucking here?

NATE   Josh is raging.
        Pacing.
        The damp night air, steaming around him.
        I slowly manoeuvres Freckles' head off my shoulder
        I stands up.

YAZ   I'm looking for my phone in my bag.
        I text Samantha.
        Tell her who I'm with.

NATE   You're gonna have to calm it down mate or you're
        gonna do some serious damage to your leg.
        He comes at me.
        Puts his forehead on my head.

JOSH   Don't fucking tell me what to do.

NATE   I've seen this a million times with a million
Josh Taylors.
I'm calm.
But his behaviour's noted.
I never took him for a peacock.
Alright mate.
Alright.

JOSH   Fucking grime.

YAZ   Samantha texts me back to get pictures.

JOSH   The state of her
Look at her.

YAZ   Hey!

NATE   I'm gonna get you home Josh.
You seem a bit tired and emotional there.

JOSH   I could have her right now and she'd let me.

YAZ   Could you fuck.

JOSH   Right here in the middle of the high street.

NATE   I don't know what's going on with you mate.

JOSH   What I don't understand is you got a wife waiting for
you at home.
A good woman.
The mother of your kids.
And you're down in the gutter, jumping on that.

YAZ   What the fuck is your problem? You don't know me.

JOSH   What happened to doing the right thing by
another person.
Loyalty.

NATE   I'm a bit baffled by this, if I'm honest cos I been
looking out for you. I'm showing you the way.
That's how we do it.
That's how I been brought up that is.
To look out for my mates.
What's mine is yours, yours is mine.

You know this. This is our world.
I was hoping we was getting somewhere, me and you.
Cos I rate you. I really rate you.
But if you're gonna dog me out every time you has
a shot or two, then I ain't gonna lie,
that's gonna be a problem for me.

JOSH   A black cab with a light on top is waiting at the traffic
        lights fifty yards away.
        As Nate lectures me on some bullshit man code, I raise
        my hand.
        Yell at it.
        I see my club's colours on the driver's shirt
        Sorted
        And right here
        Right now
        All I want to do is go home.
        Cos I don't want to see Meg leave
        Cos I'm scared of what I'd see
        Scared of who she'd leave with
        And what that would do to me
        And what I'd do because of it
        Slowly the cab draws into the curbside,
        The window lowers.
        A handful of clubbers barter me for the ride.
        But I know,
        He's a Raven.
        There's only one fare this prick is interested in.

YAZ   Tony.
        Like a big fat, Lionel Richie-loving, guardian angel.
        One time right, I watched this film and it had an angel
        in it called Clarence and looking at Tony now it
        crosses my mind that they might be the same person.
        Or angel.
        Tony is my Clarence.
        Josh Taylor is giving it the Big 'I Am', swatting away
        competition for the cab like flies.
        He leans in
        Tony nods towards me.
        Josh is begging, all palms up and pleading.

Tony insists.
Pointing at me.
He is a diamond.
A big sort of blingy, chunky, twenty-carat, no-legs,
diamond.

NATE   I sit in the back of the cab next to Josh and tells him
         we're going on to the hotel.
         The crew are up for an after-party.
         Lined up some girls.
         Why don't he come?

JOSH   I lean my head into the cold window of the taxi.
         And as we pull away
         I see her
         My Meg
         Meg,
         I shouts out,
         starts to slide down the window,
         Over here.
         My voice is lost in the street
         She turns around
         Turns away from me
         Behind her
         The mug she was with on the dance floor
         Not much to him
         Skinny and floppy hair
         He puts his arm around her shoulders
         Kisses the top of her head
         Familiar
         She looks giddy
         With him
         Puts her arms around his waist
         Her head turns in my direction and for a moment we
         lock eyes
         But the ache in my chest tells me I lost her.
         I push it down, the ache.
         Push it away with hate.
         Look away with the same hate
         Turns out she's a slag an' all.
         They all fucking are.

Bitch.
I turn to Nate.
Yeah, alright, I says, I'm up for a nightcap.

YAZ   Tony's not happy with the hotel situation. There's
a surprise.
Not happy at all.
He says he'll take me home.
He just took my brother and Samantha back – double
surprise
I tell him I'm not going home.
Not tonight.
I'm not going back there to listen to them two
shagging tonight.
And fuck it.
You Only Live Once.
And it's not every day you get the chance to spend the
night with one of the Ravens.
And it ain't just any one of them.

It's Nate West.
My Mr Snow.

I tell him he's getting obsessive and that he needs to
get off my case.
You're not my dad or something, I tells him, so stop
acting weird.
He shakes his head,
On your head be it, he says sighing as he song blocks
me with Lionel Richie's 'Dancing on the Ceiling'.

NATE   Text. The wife. Where the fuck are you?

YAZ   Text. Samantha. Selfie. My brother's behind her in
my kitchen.

JOSH   Text. My mother. There's no milk.

NATE   Text. Me to Solo. What's the room number?

JOSH   Text. My mother. Or fags.

NATE   Text. The wife. Finger emoji.

YAZ   Text. Samantha. Where's all the johnnies gone?

NATE   Text. Solo. 107.
WhatsApp. Photo of Dano with his tongue down some girl's neck.
Solo's hand is halfway to paradise.

YAZ   Text. Me to Samantha. Going to hotel.

JOSH   Text. Meg. Where are you?

YAZ   Text. Samantha. LMFAO. He's married. You're betting on the wrong horse.

JOSH   Text. Me to Meg. Fuck you.

YAZ   Text. Samantha. Just make sure you get pictures.
I sink into Nate's shoulder and click.
Send to Samantha.

JOSH   The hotel bar is tragic.

NATE   I get a bottle of fizz. Tell Joshie to get the room key from reception.

JOSH   Nate means well. He does. He really does.

YAZ   I'm starving. Like eat-a-scabby-horse starving.

NATE   Josh comes back with the key. Hands it to me.

YAZ   I grab handfuls of peanuts from a bowl at the bar.

JOSH   I buy a bottle of whiskey, take a seat in the bar and get started on my journey to oblivion
Solo and Dano roll in
Sandwiched between three girls
Tits and legs
Full of themselves
Dano is chanting 'after-party' and jumping from chair to chair
Solo gets them in
The bar manager tells Dano he's gonna have to keep it down what with this being a Thursday an' all
Dano parks himself in a corner and pats his thighs, 'room for two'
And the last one cracks on with that muppet.
He nods to Solo

Who frisbees a beer mat back and pisses himself when
it lands in a random guy's pint.
Whiskey.

YAZ   Champagne.
Photo.
Send it to Samantha.

JOSH   A boring geezer in a cheap suit inserts himself next to
me while I'm waiting for Nate
I pour a dram.
He's been coming to this hotel for twenty years.
Another dram.
Once a month
On his firm
They tried to put him up in the Premier Inn
There was talk of cuts
But quality for him is non-negotiable
Don't get him wrong
He's not a snob
But he likes the finer things in life
Food, wine, women
Another dram
And another
And another
Another.

YAZ   Two girls I don't know are sat on Nate's mate, Dano.
Pretending they're interested.
Half-heartedly laughing and playing with him.
But their eyes are on Josh.
He's the prize.
Angry and beautiful.
The keeper of secrets.
He's not playing.
They get off Dano and start dancing a bit.
Grinding.
Leaning in to each other and whispering.
One of them glances over at Nate and runs her tongue
across her lip.
I feel Nate's hand inching its way up my thigh.
I watch his hand

he's wearing a wedding band.
Gold and cold.
Catching the yellow lighting of the hotel bar
Getting closer to where I want it to be
I imagine his wife at home,
Sat in one of the huge houses overlooking the bay
She'll have a good life, everything she wants
Everything I want.
For a second I consider whether I care about her
As his fingers reach the top of my thighs
I realise that I don't
All's fair
At that moment, I realise that all I care about is me
What I want
All I care about is him
Not about him
About fucking him
THE Nate West fucking me
That's what I want
Right now
The girls are watching him as they dance the music's
stopped but still they grind
One of them gets her phone out and faces it at us
I take Nate's hand and move it inside my pants.
I want her to see he's with me.
I lean in to him and whisper in his ear.
How hard are you?
Hard.
How hard?
Really fucking hard.
I want you to fuck me.
Now.

NATE   The room is basic.
        We don't make it to the bed.
        The first time.
        We only just make it to the room.
        We don't close the door.
        No clothes removed
        No time
        I take her against the wall.

It's quick.
She wanted it quick.
Fast.
Faster.
A guy walks past the door
He's in a uniform.
Works at the hotel.
A porter or something.
I let him watch for a bit before
I kick the door shut with my foot.
Harder
Faster
Fuck me
Fuck
Fuck me
She comes.
After.
When we're finished.
We're on the floor.
She crawls to the bed.
I follow her.
Trousers by my knees
Acting like a restraint.
We laugh about that.
I pull her knickers off with my teeth.
I fight with my jeans.
Tugging them off.
Trapped by a belt.
I pull that off.
We laugh.
We lay on the bed together and laugh.
After the first time.
She turns to me.
I'm hungry, she says.
Thirsty.
Help yourself, I show my dick to her.
We laugh again.
She stands.
Wobbles a bit.
Goes to the mini-bar.
Helps herself.

There's nothing to eat.
Again, I show my dick to her.
She giggles.
Freckles.
Come here.
I'm starving, she says.
She pulls down her skirt
Straightens her top.

YAZ   I need to eat.
        I'm fucked.

JOSH   Where the fuck is Nate?
        Nate.
        Fucking Nate.
        Boring geezer's shirt is pulling tight over his gut
        Some shit cover of Pink 'What About Us' is on low
        Distorting and mixing with the bullshit that's coming
        out of his mouth.
        I don't hear him any more.
        I focus on the fat that overspills his collar.
        I'm wasted.

        I see Nate's girl walking down the corridor
        She looks as pissed as I feel.
        Orders chips.
        Room 107.
        Your missus was asking after you.
        Solo's shouting over.
        At first I don't know he's shouting at me.
        She wanted to know where you was going?
        Me?
        Yeah you. Who else am I talking to?
        Who was asking after me?
        Your girl.
        Meg?
        That's the one.
        Saw you going off in the cab with Nate.
        Yeah?
        I told her we was coming here, told her you went
        home. Cos that's what I thought.
        She was with some dude.

My Meg.
Mate, she was getting in a taxi with him last I saw.
Nate's girl stumbles into a table of drinks.
Glasses smash
Drinks splash
I tell her to go back to the room but she's all about
her chips.
I pick her up
Banging on about the chips
I'll bring them, I tell her.
Room 107

NATE   Text. Josh. She's wasted mate. A mess.

JOSH   Text. Nate. That's how I like them. LOL.

NATE   Text. Josh. She ordered chips. I'm bringing them.

JOSH   Text. Nate. I got plenty for her to eat right here.
Hashtag prime fuck. Hashtag still got it.

NATE   Text. Josh. When's she going?

JOSH   Text. Nate. Join the party. I'll start her up. This one
fucking loves it.

NATE   Text. Josh. No, I'm wasted man. How the fuck you still
going? I need to sleep.

JOSH   Text. Nate. You need to get head, mate, that's what you
need. LMAO.

NATE   Text. Josh. I got the chips. On my way.

JOSH   The room is in darkness apart from the illuminations
from the telly which flicker and contrast, intermittently
across the bed.
When I first see Nate he's stood at the end of the bed.
The girl is on all fours and Nate is fucking her.
They're naked.
For a minute I don't think they know I'm there
I watch and listen.
She moans with pleasure.
Nate keeps fucking her.
I watch.

Her arms loosen and her face slowly sinks into the bed.
He pushes her head down.
Her face turned towards me
Her mouth is open, a frozen smile and her eyes are
closed.
She moans again.
Nate looks like he could go on all night.
The door clicks shut behind me and she half-opens
her eyes.
Sees me for a second.
Closes her eyes again and moans.
Puts her fingers to her head
Nate catches my eye.
Sniggers.
Nods me over.
Again she opens her eyes a bit
Peeking through her fingers
Giggles, I think
Sinks her head back down
Grabs at the sheet with a fist
Fucked, she mumbles, I don't
I'm fucked
Nate pulls out and signals over to me
Offers her to me
In that moment
In that one moment
I follow my cock
Pushing hard against my jeans
Planning its escape
I take Nate up on his offer
Take over where he left off
Close my eyes
And think of nothing
Fuck her
I fuck her
Lost in her
Lost in the moment
Lost
Nate is talking at her
Freckles

I open my eyes
He's in front of her
He's in her mouth
She stops and looks back at me
Eyes wide open
Still I fuck her.
He moves her head back.
Nate catches my eye, laughs over at me
Good fucking times, he laughs.
The television turns his smile silver
then electric blue
I hear the breath of them.
Of us.
Feel it.
Hear us.
The breath of us.
Nate comes
Makes a huge fucking song and dance about it
Lies back on the bed and sighs.
She whimpers a bit.
I look at her.
I think of Meg.
I see Meg.
Not this.
I want this over with.
I pull out.
Thirsty, she says
That whimper again.
She sniffs.
She picks herself off the bed and staggers to the toilet.
I hear the door lock.
I pull up my trousers
The taps running.
I leave.

NATE   Fifteen missed calls. The wife.
Text. The wife. What the fuck are you playing at?
Text. The wife. What the fuck is going on with you?
Text. The wife. If you're not home within the hour
then there is going to be big shit going down here.
Text. The wife. Don't fucking bother coming home.

Text. The wife. Get your arse home NOW!
The now's in CAPS.

I tap at the bathroom door.
The taps are running
And there's no answer.
Freckles?
I think the night's run its course.
Alright my darling.
Um… nice one.
I leave, settle the bill on the way out.
Get them to call me a cab.
If I get home to the missus now, it'll earn me some
Brownie points.
Damage limitation.

WhatsApp. Solo. Photo of me and Freckles in the bar.
– The happy couple. Spill.
Me to Solo. – A gentleman never tells – Try Joshie boy.
Solo. – Fuck me. Joshie got his end away an' all? You
should have called me.
Me to Solo. – Fucking riot. Epic night.

YAZ   I know I'm in the bathroom because the taps are running
The floor is cold
I like it cold.
I don't know how long I sit there but I do know, I don't
want to go back into the room.
So I stay on the cold floor.
I check the door.
It's locked.
I locked it.
I don't know why.
The taps are running.
That's good.
I'm thirsty.
I stand up.
Lean into the sink and splash cold water on my face.
And again.
I cup the water in my hand and gulp at it.
My lips suck at the water in my palm and I notice
they're sore.

I touch my lips.
There's blood.
Water.
I splash water on my face.
The cold drops drip onto my chest and I realise
I'm naked.
I look down at myself and see that I'm naked.
My skin is mottled.
Cold.
I pull at it.
My skin.
Is it my skin?
Is that my face?
I'm not sure it's me.
Blood is on my thighs.
I put my hand between my legs and realise the blood
has come from me.
I run my hands under the tap.
Everything is sore.
Hurting.
The door.
Check it's locked.
Again.
Is it locked.
I lock it again.
Check it.
Sit back on the floor.
Listen to the rush of the taps
And close my eyes.

JOSH   The taxi turns into my estate.
Zigzag lines of black and amber.
Occasional street lamps on but mainly they're
council cut.
It's quiet.
Still.
Mostly people are asleep.
Locked tight in their boxes.
The shaft of headlamps illuminates the road ahead
A fox crosses into a garden carrying an empty
hot-dog tin.

He stops and turns his head into the taxi's light
Eyes neon, wild, unsure if he's been caught
My phone buzzes in my pocket
The night tries to fight its way into my thoughts
I push it away
We pull up in my street.
Anywhere by yer, drive.
He stops a few doors down and I get out.
Tap his roof and turn towards my house.
She's standing.
Wiping off her arse from the cold step.
Walking towards me.
Heels clicking, echoing in the silence of the night.
She stands in front of me.
Looking down.
She sniffs.
I lift her chin.
And even though we been looking at each other since
we was kids,
we look at each other now, like it's the first time we
ever seen each other.
Meg.
She kisses me.
Like I'm home.
And I kiss her back.

YAZ   When I wake up the room is silent.
I stand and listen at the door.
After a while I unlock it
I'm alone
In the room
It's daylight.
I'm naked.
I look around.
I don't feel right
In my core.
My clothes are scattered.
I pick them up
Pull them on.
Look around for my bag.
My legs are shaking.

I try to piece together last night.
Everything is hurting.
I remember the bar
And Nate
Champagne
I empty my bag on the messed-up bedsheets
Pick out my phone
Dial for Tony.
Come and get me.
Hurry.
Hurry, Tony please.
Please.
He's outside the hotel within five minutes.
As I get in the car, I warn him I'm not in the mood.
Then I sit next to him and sob.
He doesn't say anything as he drives.
But he passes me a custard cream and a tissue.
And instead of taking me home he pulls up outside the
police station.
We sit there for hours.
And I tell him
I don't even know.
I can't remember.
Not properly.
I know something happened
And I know it weren't right
He sits quietly.
Breathing deeply.
They'll think it's my fault.
No, he says, No, don't you think that.
It's what they'll think, I says
It's what everyone will think.
Look at me, I'm a fuck-up.
That's not what I see kid, he says.
Don't talk like that about yourself.
And then in anger Tony takes off his red and black
Ravens' shirt
And spits on it
Throws it out of the window
And he sits there

In his vest
With his moobs
And I giggle and cry all at the same time
And then
I can't. I say, I just can't. I'm sorry Tone.
Then
Tony tells me this isn't the first time
And it won't be the last
He's been in the taxi game for thirty-five years
And it's always been the same
Then he clicks on Lionel Richie,
And we sit there
'Sail On'
And we sit and we listen
And the words don't mean anything
But they mean everything
For unknown reasons
Sitting here with the Commodores
This means everything
And Tony sings
Loud and out of tune
Sail on.
He turns it up
And he closes his eyes

Sings the refrain from 'Sail On' by Lionel Richie.

I close my eyes too
And I sing
And then I open the door
I get out of the car
Straighten myself up
and I walk into the station.

The End.

A Nick Hern Book

Lose Yourself first published in Great Britain in 2019 as a paperback original by Nick Hern Books Limited, The Glasshouse, 49a Goldhawk Road, London W12 8QP, in association with Sherman Theatre, Cardiff

Lose Yourself copyright © 2019 Katherine Chandler

Katherine Chandler has asserted her moral right to be identified as the author of this work

Cover image: Burning Red

Designed and typeset by Nick Hern Books, London
Printed in the UK by Mimeo Ltd, Huntingdon, Cambridgeshire PE29 6XX

A CIP catalogue record for this book is available from the British Library

ISBN 978 1 84842 865 2

CAUTION All rights whatsoever in this play are strictly reserved. Requests to reproduce the text in whole or in part should be addressed to the publisher.

Amateur Performing Rights Applications for performance, including readings and excerpts, by amateurs in the English language throughout the world should be addressed to the Performing Rights Manager, Nick Hern Books, The Glasshouse, 49a Goldhawk Road, London W12 8QP, *tel* +44 (0)20 8749 4953, *email* rights@nickhernbooks.co.uk, except as follows:

Australia: Dominie Drama, 8 Cross Street, Brookvale 2100, *tel* (2) 9938 8686, *fax* (2) 9938 8695, *email* drama@dominie.com.au

New Zealand: Play Bureau, PO Box 9013, St Clair, Dunedin 9047, *tel* (3) 455 9959, *email* info@playbureau.com

United States of America and Canada: Curtis Brown Ltd, see details below.

Professional Performing Rights Application for performance by professionals in any medium and in any language throughout the world should be addressed to Curtis Brown Ltd, Haymarket House, 28–29 Haymarket, London SW1Y 4SP, *tel* +44 (0)20 7393 4400, *fax* +44 (0)20 7393 4401, *email* cb@curtisbrown.co.uk

No performance of any kind may be given unless a licence has been obtained. Applications should be made before rehearsals begin. Publication of this play does not necessarily indicate its availability for amateur performance.

www.nickhernbooks.co.uk

facebook.com/nickhernbooks

twitter.com/nickhernbooks